# Longer
# FLY CASTING

**BOOKS BY LEFTY KREH**

**Longer Fly Casting**

**Fly Fishing in Salt Water**

**Practical Fishing Knots**
*(with Mark Sosin)*

**Fly Casting with Lefty Kreh**

**Salt Water Fly Patterns**

# Longer
# FLY CASTING

## LEFTY KREH

The Lyons Press

Printed in the United States of America
10 9

Library of Congress Cataloging-in-Publication Data

Kreh, Lefty.
Longer fly casting / Lefty Kreh; illustrated by Rod
Walinchus.
p.     cm.
Includes index.
ISBN 1-55821-127-6: $12.95
1. Fly casting.   I. Title.
SH454.2.K72   1991
799.1'2—dc20      91-30223
CIP

# CONTENTS

# Publisher's Preface

I never met a fly fisherman who did not want to be able to cast ten feet—or more—farther. The trout or tarpon or permit or bass always seem *at least* that distance beyond our best cast, and there is simply no adequate solution other than being able to make a longer cast.

Sometimes you may have plenty of room to engineer such longer casts—if you know how; but often, "longer" means ten feet added to a forty-foot roll cast or to some special cast determined by sharply restricted surroundings.

Of course we sometimes need more than ten feet to do the business at hand—and perhaps in the end what we really want are *principles* by which we can continue to lengthen our casts over a period of many years, through thoughtful practice. For one of the great pleasures a lot of us take in all aspects of fly fishing is that we never learn it all, and always want to learn a little more.

This little handbook, graced with Rod Walinchus's clear drawings, will help you to refine your fly casting—to cast with more accuracy and authority but primarily for greater distance. It is a short, narrowly focused book, but an important one, we think—one that establishes principles to live with along with specific techniques. We hope you'll find Lefty an ebullient, innovative, and skillful teacher.

NICK LYONS

# Longer
# FLY CASTING

# 1

## Getting More Distance
## Out of Your Casts

For several hundred years, one method of fly casting has dominated the sport—that of duplicating the sweep of the hands on a clock face with the casting motions. This method also involves moving the rod through a relatively short arc. Let's look at how this method—so universal today—was developed.

Several centuries ago in Europe, anglers began using artificial flies, rather than live bait, to catch trout. Their tackle was crude. A long, often sixteen-foot, wooden rod, to which was attached several feet of braided horsehair and a short gut leader, allowed them to cast their flies across narrow streams. They determined that, with a long rod, if they started at about belt level with the rod tip (nine on the clock face) and swept up swiftly, stopping at about the twelve or one o'clock position, they could make an effective cast for the conditions they encountered. Until the middle of this century, casting instructors often had students hold a book under the elbow of the casting arm—in order not to drop the book, the caster had to limit the arc of his swing to within the nine-to-one area.

The book technique is no longer used, of course, but we are still teaching a method that was developed several centuries ago for conditions few modern anglers face. Tackle has changed dramatically. We no longer cast just on narrow meadow streams. Instead, we throw flies across wide steelhead and salmon rivers. We thrust a bonefish fly or bass bug into a stiff breeze. Those seeking billfish with a fly rod frequently are casting flies that are longer than some of the trout caught by those Europeans who developed the nine-to-one-o'clock method.

Yet, and perhaps because fly fishing is so bound by tradition, we have not brought any real changes to that basic casting technique developed so long ago.

The method I have been advocating and teaching for many years is totally different from the conventional, centuries-old way. But let me first emphasize that the nine-to-one-o'clock method *will* allow a good caster to obtain long distances, and even throw large flies. But it requires a great deal more energy and effort than the method I suggest. Not only will you get more distance and easier casting with my method, but older folks, women, and people not possessing great strength can cast for considerable distances and long periods of time without tiring when using it. Both methods work. But mine will do the job easier, and will allow you to throw farther with less effort—and you will become a more accomplished caster faster than you would if you learned the older style.

With the modern method I urge you to try, you need learn only five basic principles to make any practical cast. Once you understand these five principles, you can also evaluate your casting. Being able to critique your own casting is extremely valuable when you try to improve.

## LEFTY'S METHOD OF CASTING

I believe that when using the conventional, less-efficient, style of casting, the double haul acts as a crutch. Once you master the method I suggest and then learn the double haul, longer casts will come much easier. My method does not refer at all to the clock face, and it asks you to discard much of what you have been taught about the traditional way to cast. Those who have never been exposed to conventional fly casting pick up my method quickly and do well. Those who have been using the conventional style of casting will find that they must forget many of the precepts of that style. Let's begin by examining my five principles of casting.

**PRINCIPLE NUMBER ONE The longer you move the rod through an arc, the more it helps you make the cast.**

Your rod is nothing more than a flexible lever. The longer that lever moves during the cast, the more it contributes to the length of the cast—and the less work you have to put into it. The conventional method doesn't allow you to move the rod very far, and because it involves so little movement of the lever, anyone who wants to cast a longer distance has to resort to a technique called the double haul. The conventional method is so inefficient that a double haul is necessary to obtain *any* distance.

One of the major differences between my method and the conventional style is that for more difficult or longer casts, I urge casters to move the rod well behind the body on the backcast. Remember, the longer you move a rod through an arc, the more it helps on the cast. For a short cast there is no need to go way back, but as longer casts are needed, the rod is moved progressively farther back. For example, when casting only fifteen to thirty feet, there is no need to take the rod even as far as the shoulder. But if a longer cast is desired, you may want to reach a little farther back, and on a very long cast your rod and arm should be straight behind you.

**PRINCIPLE NUMBER TWO** You must get the line end moving before you can make a back or a forward cast. And on the backcast, the end of the line must be lifted from the water before making the cast.

Many instructors tell you that you should make your backcast at nine or ten or ten-thirty on the clock face, regardless of where the line is. I don't care what time it is, you can't make a cast in either direction until you get the end of the line moving. It doesn't have to be moving toward you, but you *must* get it in motion. On the backcast, water tension grips the line and doesn't want to release it, which is why it's so important to lift the rod high enough that you free the line from the water before making the cast. This is especially critical when trying to lift a lot of line off the surface. Because the line is already in the air during most forward casts, you need only move the rod enough to get the entire line in motion before you cast.

**PRINCIPLE NUMBER THREE** The fly is going to go in the direction that you accelerate, then stop, the rod tip at the end of the cast.

This is one of the most important principles to understand about casting. Once understood, it will allow you to throw accurate casts, or that desirable curve to the left or right, and help you analyze what you are doing right and wrong. *Only that brief acceleration at the end of the cast determines the direction and flight of the fly.*

**PRINCIPLE NUMBER FOUR** The size of the line loop during the cast is determined by how fast and how far the rod tip is moved (com-bined with a quick stop) at the end of the cast.

If you sweep the rod forward and accelerate quickly at the end of your cast, so that the tip moves through a four-foot arc, you will throw a four-foot-high loop. If you accelerate the rod tip through an arc of only a foot, you will throw a one-foot loop. Once this principle is mastered, you can create any size loop you want.

For distance casting, small loops are always desirable. Many people think a wide loop doesn't go as far as a narrow or tight loop because of air resistance. Actually, air resistance has very little to do with it. The reason a big loop doesn't go anywhere is because the angler is throwing the force of his cast around a curve or arc. The caster throwing a tight loop is throwing most of his line and energy *at* the target.

Using your wrist to help make casts will cause you to throw wide, open loops. To demonstrate this for yourself, take the tip section of a fly rod and hold its lower end in your casting hand. Come forward slowly, as if you were making a forward cast. Now accelerate your rod hand only four inches. Be sure to keep your wrist locked, and make the accelerated movement only with your forearm. Do this several times and you'll see that the rod tip moves a short distance (which is the size of the loop that unrolls toward the target). Now repeat the motion, but this time bend your wrist, as most casters do when they make a power stroke. You will see that the rod tip moves over a three- or four-times-greater arc. That causes you to throw a loop that is three or four times larger.

With considerable practice, many casters have learned to control their wrist movements, so that they don't make large loops. If you want to tighten your loops, try casting with your wrist locked. Unless you are already highly skilled, this will be your biggest step toward improving your fly casting and obtaining more distance.

**PRINCIPLE NUMBER FIVE** You cannot move your rod hand well behind the body if you begin the cast with your thumb positioned on top of the rod. You must grip the rod in a normal manner and then rotate your thumb about forty-five degrees away from your body.

With the thumb on top of the rod, your arm stops at a vertical point, about twelve o'clock, when you move it straight up and back. Try holding the rod in a normal fashion for beginning a backcast, with your thumb on top of the rod handle. Rotate your thumb outward at about a forty-five-degree angle away from your body. Move your forearm upward and backward, and you'll see that your hand can travel in a straight path well behind your body. *This is the key to getting the rod hand well back. Unless you tilt your thumb outward, your rod cannot travel 180 degrees from the target to get your rod hand straight behind you for the extra-long cast.*

The first four of these principles apply to any method of casting you choose. The fifth allows you greater freedom of rod movement when you need it. Master these principles and you'll cast farther, easier, more accurately, and will know why you are casting improperly—and how to correct it.

## PICTURING THE PRINCIPLES
*Lefty's Method—A Side View*

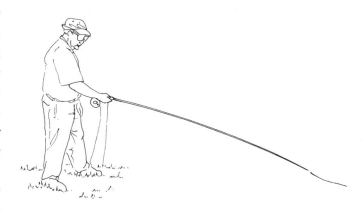

**STEP 1** For a short cast where the rod hand will be brought up only to the front of the shoulder, the thumb remains on the top of the rod handle on the backcast. But here I want to demon-

strate a longer cast, so the thumb rotates away from the body at about a forty-five-degree angle.

Footwork is important in casting. You should always place forward the foot that is opposite the hand you are using: A right-hander positions his left foot forward, and vice versa. This allows the body to move fluidly during the cast.

The rod is pointed down: Always keep the rod tip well below the belt to begin longer casts. *The thumb and forearm are rotated away from the body about forty-five degrees.*

**STEP 2** When your rod hand and forearm are rotated outward forty-five degrees, the arm brings the rod back at the angle that will be used to direct the backcast. A high backcast means the forearm will travel upward and back; a low backcast requires the forearm to travel

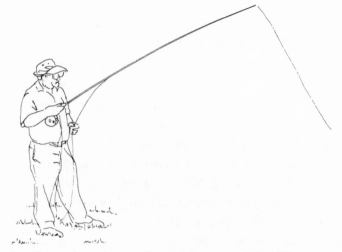

backward at a much narrower angle. The narrower the angle at which your arm travels up and back, the farther back you can reach, and the longer a cast you can make. For a very long cast, the angle will be so narrow that you'll almost be making a sidearm cast.

The wrist must not be bent at any point during the cast, and the backcast is made using

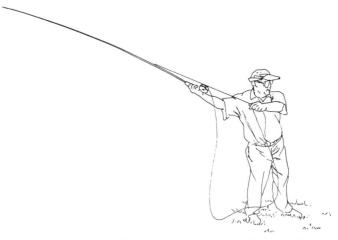

only the hand and forearm. *If the entire arm, from shoulder to wrist, were used for the backcast, the line would travel up and back in a large circle—dissipating the energy of the cast.*

Don't hold your forearm rigidly against your body. In the cast it should work much as it does when you lift a glass of water from a counter to your lips—using the elbow as a hinge, without any upper-arm movement except to accomodate the backward reach.

The final point to remember in this step is that the most effective backcast is the one that travels directly away from the target, at 180 degrees. If it's thrown in any other direction, you must redirect it before you'll be able to deliver the fly to the target—and that redirection will mean a loss of energy to the cast. For a long cast, always try to throw your backcast 180 degrees from the target.

**STEP 3** Another difference between this method and the conventional style is that you do not "drift" the rod after you begin the cast. You decide how far back you want to go on the backcast, and you move rather swiftly upward to near that stopping point. Then, make the shortest and swiftest acceleration *in the direction you want the fly and line to go* and abruptly stop the rod. Remember, the size of a loop in front or back is determined by how fast and how far you move the rod tip at the end of the cast, *combined with a quick stop*. This is not a power stroke but a quick acceleration of the forearm. And because the wrist has not been used, it is much easier to move the rod this way, especially a heavy one. The line will move in the direction at which the rod tip is pointing when you stop. If the line travels at an angle behind you, or dips toward the water or ground, it is because you stopped the rod tip while it was pointing in that direction. *It is vital that on the acceleration backward you move swiftly and stop the rod tip in the direction you want the line to travel.*

**STEP 4** On a long cast the arm will be fully extended to the rear, but with the upper arm still below the shoulder! Ideally, at this point you should be able to look down a straight line con-

sisting of your arm, the rod, and the line. You will lean back on the foot that is on the same side as your rod arm. The longer the cast, the farther back you lean. This will allow you to move the rod through a long arc.

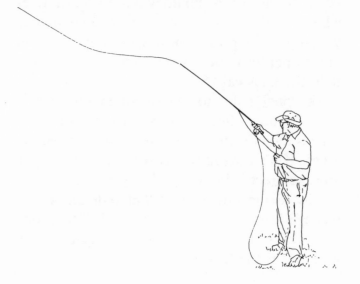

from you, and the upward-moving rod, when it hits the unrolling line, will help straighten the line and load the rod. If you wait until you feel a tug on the rod on the backcast, before you can move the rod forward the backward-moving line will already have tugged, straightened, and started to fall. That's like shooting at a duck where he is—not where he's going to be.

**STEP 5** To begin the forward cast, bring your rod forearm around and in toward your body, so that your thumb is pointing up. Don't wait for the line to unroll completely; if you do, you'll waste good casting energy. When your line looks like a candy cane or a J, move the rod forward. The line will be unrolling away

**STEP 6** Continue to move your forearm—and *only* your forearm—toward the target, making sure your upper arm stays below your shoulder. *There is never a time in casting when the upper arm should be level with the shoulder.* Holding the upper arm as higher or higher than the shoulder can result in many casting problems. It takes a superior caster to keep the upper arm elevated and still make a good cast.

Remember to keep your wrist straight.

**STEPS 7 AND 8** When you can see your rod hand with your peripheral vision while looking at the target, it is time to accelerate—swift and short—in the direction you want the line to go. The cast should be directed almost straight at the target. However, if you do that and let the tip remain where you stopped it, a tailing loop is almost sure to result. To prevent tailing

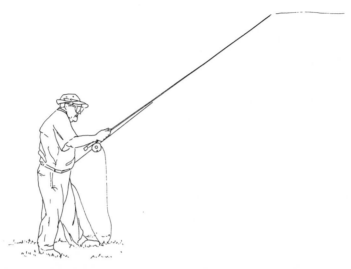

loops, the instant you stop toward the target, dip the rod only enough to know that you have moved the handle. I tell people to tilt the thumb downward just a frog's hair. The slightest movement of the rod hand will mean considerable movement at the end of the rod; tilt the thumb down too much and you'll drag the loop open and spoil the cast.

Don't lower the rod to the fishing position immediately. If you do, you'll pull the loop open. Once the unrolling loop is a rod length forward of the tip, you can lower the rod. An easy way to determine when you can do this is to make the stop and count a quick one-two-three, then drift the rod tip downward.

### Lefty's Method—A Front View

In my method, the angle at which the rod travels is slightly different from the conventional style. On short casts, the thumb is on top of the rod handle, and the rod comes almost straight back. But on longer casts, the backcast is more of a sidearm cast only because the forearm can be moved in a straight line to well behind the body when doing this. Study the head-on as well as the side views in the drawings to see what I mean.

**STEP 1** The forearm is rotated outward from the body about forty-five degrees, and the rod tip is pointing at the target and held very low. See how the reel is tilted at an angle. It will remain at that angle throughout the backcast.

you want the line to travel. Note that the rod is still angled off to the side.

**STEP 2** For optimum efficiency, the rod must travel 180 degrees away from the target on the backcast. Note that the forearm is used only to throw the cast, and that the upper arm just follows along naturally. The rod is brought quickly upward and directly away from the target. Brief acceleration is then made at the angle at which

**STEP 3** As soon as the backcast is made, the rod hand is brought around and in toward the body—*it travels in an oval*—and then moves straight toward the target.

**STEP 4** The forward cast is made. What is important to understand from this front view is that the rod will travel in a side cast until the end of the backcast. Then it is brought around and straight forward. Viewed from overhead, the rod travels in a definite oval during the cast.

*The conventional cast and how the hand travels during it*

**STEP 1** The conventional method of casting requires that the thumb be held on top of the rod, as shown.

**STEP 2** If the thumb remains on top of the rod handle on the backcast the hand can travel only this far before the body blocks further movement. This limits the distance you can move the rod back in a straight line.

*The Effects of Bending and Not Bending
the Wrist*

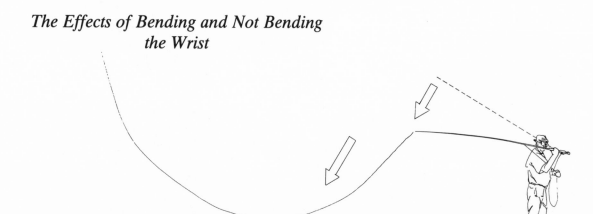

**VIEW 1** The conventional method asks you to bend your wrist to create a power stroke that throws the line at the target. My method advocates no "power" application, only a quick acceleration at the end of the cast. This drawing demonstrates how bending the wrist at the end of the cast develops wide loops and unwanted slack in the line.

Principle Number 2 says that the line is going to go in the direction that the rod tip is pointed when it stops. If the wrist is bent at the end of the backcast, as shown in the drawing, the line is going to travel down and back. That means that most of your forward rod motion will contribute nothing toward throwing the fly toward its target because of the pull of that slack. You cannot make a forward cast until you remove that deep sag in the line behind you.

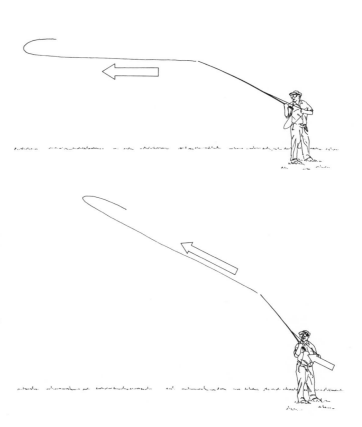

**VIEWS 2 AND 3** If the forearm and hand are stopped, with the wrist locked, after accelerating in a straight back-and-upward direction, the line will travel straight behind. There is no slack, so any forward movement of the rod will instantly begin moving all of the line and fly toward the target.

Loop size is determined by the distance the rod tip moves when accelerated at the end of the backcast. If the wrist bends, the tip travels over a much longer arc and the loop size increases.

# 2

## The Double Haul

Just about every advanced fly caster uses the double haul. Some anglers who cast a long line using the double haul would be very hard pressed to cast even a moderately long line without using it. Perhaps the greatest mistake made by most casters is that they learn the double haul too soon.

It is important to understand that the double haul only makes the line go faster—it doesn't necessarily make you a better caster. What should be learned first is to cast with good technique. Then learn the double haul. Most fishermen use the double haul to throw their casting mistakes faster over a longer distance.

I can't stress enough that good casting technique should be mastered before you learn to double-haul. It is important to realize that once the line straightens on the cast or completes unrolling, it falls. No matter how far you cast, once that line straightens, the cast ends. When not using the double haul, what makes one cast go farther than another is the distance and speed with which the rod is accelerated, coupled with a quick stop. The shorter the distance you accelerate, and the faster your rod hand travels during that acceleration and then stops, the tighter will be the loop and the farther the line will go.

As explained in Principle Number 4, the faster you accelerate the rod tip, and the quicker you stop it, wiil determine how far the line will travel—if a small loop is formed. When you double haul, you accelerate the rod tip's speed and that increases the speed of the line flight. *Therefore, it is important not to make long pulls during a double haul.*

If you make a short acceleration with your rod hand and stop quickly, you have performed the cast correctly. But if you then make a long haul with your line hand, you restrict the sudden stop of the rod and reduce distance. *The best motion for a double haul is for you to move the line hand the same distance as you move the rod hand during the acceleration.* This causes the rod tip to accelerate faster and stop quicker. If you want to be a great double-hauler, *don't make long pulls!*

It behooves the caster to learn first how to accelerate a short distance and come to a quick stop. That way, he learns to make efficient casts where the line is going to go a long way before it unrolls or straightens. Then, if the double haul is added, the caster really can do wondrous things.

Let's examine how most people double-haul—and why they are inefficient in executing it.

**STEP 1** If you watch most double-haulers, you'll see that they yank downward with the rod hand on the back and forward casts. They make such long hauls that they must surely sometimes tear their underwear. But I believe long pulls are detrimental to good double-hauling for several reasons. This drawing shows the length some anglers pull on a haul.

**STEP 2** One of the problems associated with extra-long pulls is shown in this drawing. At the end of the backcast, as the rod drifts forward, the line wraps around the base of the rod or the reel, spoiling the forward cast. To prevent the line wrapping around the rod butt, the line hand should always be eighteen inches or closer to the reel. It is when the rod and line hands are separated widely that tangles occur. A much shorter pull or haul eliminates this problem.

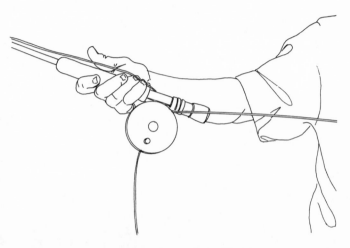

Another problem with the longer haul is that most anglers haul violently down and outward from the body with the line hand. This often causes the rod tip to recoil in the opposite direction, and the line is forced to the outside on the backcast instead of going directly backward. For example, a right-hander might pull down and to the left on the first haul. That causes the rod tip to recoil to the right. This makes the tip throw the line out to the right as it travels back, reducing line speed on the cast. By pulling directly away from and in line with the rod, the tip recoils opposite the direction of pull and helps you make an even faster backcast.

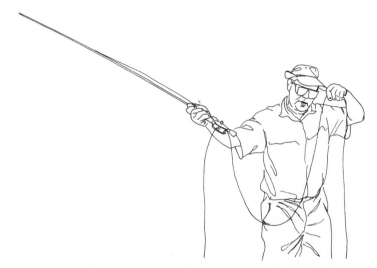

**STEP 3** If a long haul is made on the backcast, the angler is going to have to make another haul on the forward cast. The long haul pulled the two hands well apart, but now the line hand must be brought back near the rod hand for the second haul. This coming together of the two hands (the rod is also moving forward) creates a lot of slack, which has to be removed either with part of the haul or with additional rod motion before the forward cast can be made. Remember Principle Number 2: You must get the line end moving before you can make a cast in front or back.

## THE CORRECT METHOD FOR MAKING THE DOUBLE HAUL

To execute an efficient double haul, you need move the line hand on each haul only four or five inches or less. Longer pulls on the line lead to problems. *It is critical that the hauls be performed at exactly the same time the rod is being accelerated on the back and forward casts.* Hauls and acceleration go together. If they are performed together they're like a knockout punch, and you'll get great efficiency out of the cast.

Remember, in good double-hauling the line hand should never roam more than eighteen or twenty inches from the rod hand. The farther they get apart, the more slack is liable to accumulate, and the more difficult it will be to make an efficient cast. Long hauls can be made and a good cast completed, but this takes years of practice. Keep your hands closer together and you won't have to spend those years practicing.

On the backcast, the line hand should follow the reel. On the forward cast, the line hand should move away from the reel or precede it. Follow the rules—short hauls and line hand no more than twenty inches from the reel during the entire casting motion—and you will greatly improve your double hauls.

There is an easy method for learning the double haul, which I think is one of the few things difficult to master in casting. However, if you try to learn to make a back and a forward cast and the double haul all at once, you'll most likely get confused. Instead, by using my technique, most anglers can learn the double haul in less than half an hour of practice.

Find a large open area, perhaps your backyard, and cast a line on the grass in front of you. As you raise the rod to make a backcast, follow the reel with your line hand. Try to stay within eighteen or twenty inches of it. At *exactly the same time* that you speed up and stop, or accelerate, to throw the line behind you, tug down sharply, only a few inches, with the line hand. The two motions must be performed together for maximum efficiency: If you accelerate and tug at the same time, the line will leap behind you much faster than a normal backcast. You've just made a single haul! As soon as the tug is completed, immediately bring the line hand up close to the reel. If you only tugged a few inches, as you should have, you won't see any slack accumulated in the line between the rod hand and first rod guide.

As soon as the backcast is finished, allow the line to fall to the grass behind you. Now you have time to think about how you are going to make the forward cast and the second part of the haul. When the rod hand moves forward, the line hand should, too. Try to keep the rod and line hands moving at the same speed, so that they remain the same distance from each other during the forward movement. If you allow the line hand to move forward too far, or not come forward far enough, you will create slack that will spoil some of the cast's efficiency. When you accelerate to make the forward cast, *at the same time* give a swift three- to five-inch tug with the line hand. You have completed another single haul. If you did it correctly, the line will zip forward.

Don't rush things. Repeat the back and forward casts, and each time let the line fall to the grass. Then, think about how each cast is to be made. Once you have trained your muscles to do a single haul in each direction, make a backcast, but don't let the line fall to the grass. Instead, while it's in the air, make a forward false cast and double haul. Continue to false-cast (using the double haul) until things go awry. As soon as you have a problem, lay the line out in front of you and start over.

I have been teaching this method for some time, and I can say that many people in one session learn the double haul very well.

If you already know how to double-haul and want to improve your technique, there's another simple trick for that, too. Principle Number 1 says, "The more help you need, the longer you move the rod through an arc." If you want to improve your double haul, you don't want the rod to help you, for it will mask your problems. Instead, string up a half a rod—just the tip. Don't thread the line through the lower guide. Now try hauling with this half-rod. You'll find that so long as your line hand stays close to the rod hand and the tugs are timed with the rod's acceleration, the false-casting goes well. But start making longer hauls with the line hand, and things quickly get out of sync, and the cast suffers. By using a half-rod you exaggerate your double-haul faults, and can more quickly detect and correct them. Once you get it down with a half-rod, try it with the tip of a four-piece travel rod, if you have one.

*Practicing the Double Haul*

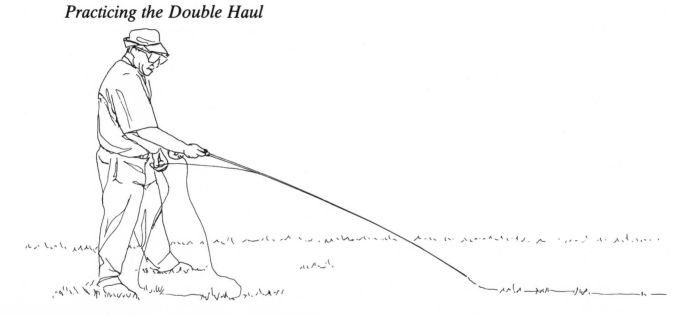

**STEP 1** Lower the rod so that the tip points at the target or fly. Remove all slack and bring the line hand to within a foot of the reel.

**STEP 2** As the rod is lifted on the backcast, your line hand "chases" the reel, staying about the same distance in relation to it as when the cast started.

**STEP 3** At the same time the rod is accelerated to throw the line back, make a short, three- to five-inch, tug on the line. Study the arrow pointing to the hand in the drawing. Note that a downward tug is made to create a single haul. The instant the tug is completed, bring the line hand back so that it is close to the reel. That way, no slack builds in the line.

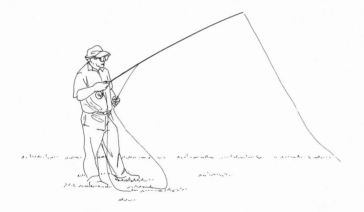

**STEP 4** Now drop the line behind you on the grass. This allows you to think a moment about the forward cast and the second haul.

**STEP 5** Bring the rod forward in preparation for the forward cast. Try to keep the rod hand and line hand close together.

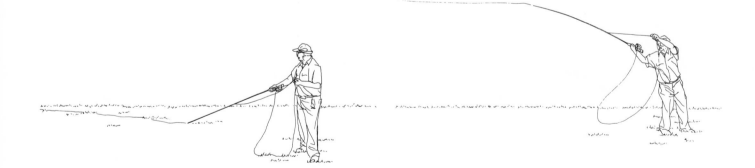

**STEP 6** As you accelerate the rod hand, tug on the line with the line hand, then return it close to the reel.

After you have practiced this exercise enough to be comfortable with it, eliminate step 4 and you're on your way to better double-hauling and greater distances in your casts.

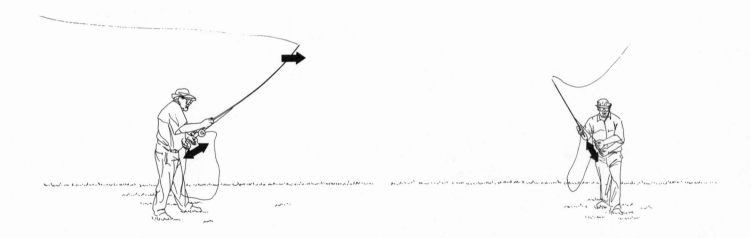

# 3

## Some Basic Tips for Longer Casts

There are a few things any fly fisher can do to help put more distance in casts.

## CLEAN LINES

Clean lines cast and shoot better. Dirt, grit, and grease that accumulate on a line create resistance when the line is shot through the guides. For that reason, anyone who desires to get maximum distance out of their casts will keep their lines super clean. There are several methods of cleaning lines. Remember that many new lines have a slick outer finish, and the use of gritty materials will sometimes spoil that finish; gentle cleaners are recommended.

One of the best ways to clean any fly line is to use warm water with a mild liquid detergent.

Saturate a sponge with the solution and then draw the line several times through the clenched sponge. It is very important to rinse all soap residue from the line—especially if it is a floating line. To do this, simply use clear cold water and draw the line a number of times through a clean sponge or rag soaked with the water.

Some anglers use a commercial vinyl cleaner called Armor All. It gives the fly line an extremely slick surface, which allows the caster to shoot a little more through the guides. The only problem is that the material is water-soluble and will wash off soon after you start fishing.

There is at least one specially designed cleaner on the market, called Glide, that has the appearance of Armor All but the characteristics of latex paint—it is water-soluble when wet, but isn't after it dries. This material is a good line-cleaner and gives fly lines a superslick coating that facilitates shooting. And it stays on the line for a considerable period of time.

There are some silicone line cleaners, too. If you use a heavy paste type, be sure to rub the line thoroughly with a dry rag after the silicone has been applied to remove as much paste as possible. If an excess is left on the line, the line will tend to pick up more dirt and will soon cast worse than it did before the silicone application.

New lines cast the best, mainly because they are clean. Don't drop your lines on dirty surfaces, and maintain a line-cleaning routine to keep your lines casting well.

## FALSE-CASTING MORE LINE

When you want to throw a longer line, one of the most important things to do is to hold more line aloft during the false cast. For example, if you want to make a ninety-foot cast, if you can false-cast sixty feet of line, you are only thirty feet short of the goal, which means you need only shoot thirty feet of the line. Any time you want to make a longer cast, try keeping a longer length of line outside the guides.

## HEAVIER LINES

When casting into a wind, many people will switch to a one-size-heavier line. For example, if they are using an 8-weight line, they will substitute a 9-weight line. But the heavier line will overload the rod tip and cause it to flex or bend deeper than normal on the cast. This will create larger line loops, which travel less distance. What should be done is to substitute a one-size *lighter* line and *false-cast more line than normal.*

The added weight of the extra amount of line being false-cast will properly load the rod without creating deeper than normal flexes or bends in the tip—that results in tight loops. And the thinner line will penetrate the wind better.

## STRIPPING-GUIDE SIZE

Another important factor in making long casts is the size of the stripping or butt guide on the fly rod. This is the lower or largest guide, nearest the handle. I once worked with a large company on the design of fly rods. I had them build me a fly-casting machine that would make a cast while we recorded the results on videotape. We learned many interesting things. One of them was that a fly line that is released from the hand to be shot toward the target does not flow in a relatively straight line. Instead, it sweeps up toward the guide in wildly wavering motions. It often strikes the butt guide and then folds over, then is drawn back, and finally slithers through. All of this is wasted energy that will detract from a cast. If you are already a person who can throw a pretty fast line, you may have experienced the line completely wrapping around the butt guide in some instances.

To alleviate this problem, it's important to install a large-diameter butt guide. For rods that throw a fly line weight 7 or larger, I urge you to have at least a sixteen-millimeter guide installed—twenty-millimeter is even better. All spinning rods have larger butt guides to gather in the wavering loops of monofilament; to a lesser degree, this is exactly what a fly rod should do.

Many rod builders know that larger guides help improve shooting line on the cast. But cosmetics plays a part in selling tackle, and few people will purchase a rod with an oversized guide. Fortunately, you can install your own or find a rod builder who can replace the too-small guide with a bigger one.

**VIEW 1** Look at the line as it wavers toward the butt guide. Note how the line tends to overlap the guide, then has to come back before it

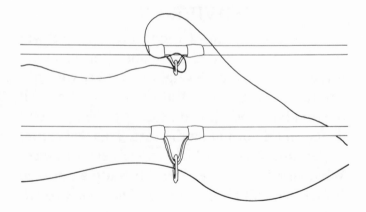

finally goes through. All of this motion steals energy from your cast.

**VIEW 2** Note how the larger guide funnels the line through better, increasing the distance of your cast.

## CASTING FORM

There are two common mistakes in casting form that detract from obtaining distance and cause other problems. The first is footwork. Some fishermen make their casts with both feet standing even. This restricts body movement. Even worse is the tendency to place forward the foot on the same side as the arm handling the rod—that is, a right-hander with his right foot forward. This restricts body movement even more.

Your body on longer casts should move well back and then forward in a smooth, fluid motion. To obtain such free movement, it's vital that the foot on the side opposite the hand using the rod (left foot forward for a right-handed caster) should be placed well in front. Ignoring this principle of good form will affect your casting distance negatively.

The second common mistake is the tendency of many casters to hold the rod-arm elbow and upper arm too high during the cast. There are several reasons why this is bad. First, when the elbow and upper arm are elevated to or higher than the shoulder, all of the arm muscles tighten. This can be very tiring after repeated casting. Second, raising the elbow higher than the shoulder restricts body movement and the ability to move smoothly. Third, with his elbow and upper arm higher than his shoulder, the an-

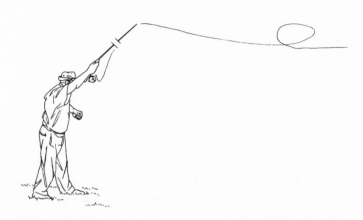

gler cannot reach well behind himself. To make a longer reach behind, he needs to sweep his arm back at a very low angle. And fourth, unless an angler is highly skilled, when he casts with the elbow as higher or higher than his shoulder, he will constantly throw tailing loops (the line or leader will tangle at the end of the cast).

# 4

## More Distance in Basic Casting Maneuvers

## CONVENTIONAL ROLL CAST

The roll cast is necessary when a backcast can't be made because of some obstruction. Unfortunately, most people make poor roll casts that result in a pile of tangled line and leader falling to the water. Two common practices result in poor roll-cast performance: Keeping the rod in front on the roll cast, and directing the end of the cast downward, causing the line to be driven down and short of the target.

Four things must be done to accomplish an efficient roll cast. First, the rod must be brought back behind the body. Remember, the longer the rod travels through an arc, the more it helps the angler. Second, the rod needs something to pull against in order to load so that it can throw the line forward. To get that tension, the line must pause so water-surface tension can grip the line. Third, the cast is going to go in the direction the rod tip is pointing when it stops, so the end of the cast must be directed toward the target—not toward the surface in front of the angler. Fourth, the size of an unrolling line loop is determined by the distance the rod tip is moved quickly and then stopped at the end of the cast. Most people make a too-long speed-and-stop motion, resulting in a loop that is too open.

### The Roll Cast

**STEP 1** To begin the roll cast, *slide* the line back slowly on the water. Don't jerk or move it too quickly. Continue to move the rod back until it is well behind your body. Remember, *the longer the cast, the farther behind the body the rod should be.* On a very long cast the rod tip would be well behind the angler and nearly parallel to the water. Allow the line to come to a stop, or pause briefly. This lets the surface

tension grab the line, so that when the rod comes forward, it has something to pull against. Stopping the line at this point is critical to good roll-casting.

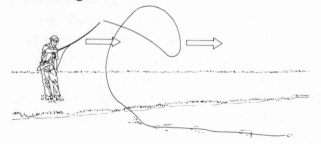

**STEP 2** *The forward roll cast should be made exactly like a conventional forward cast.* Sweep the rod forward, as in conventional casting. The faster and farther you want the cast to go, the faster and shorter the distance you must accelerate—speed up and stop—at the end of the cast.

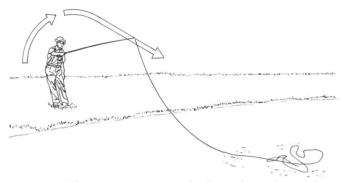

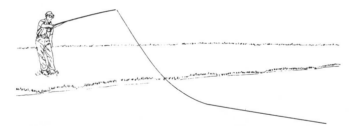

**STEP 3** *You must direct the energy or force of the cast at about eye level toward the target.* If you drive the rod downward, you will cause the cast to be directed toward the surface in front of you. As soon as the rod stops at eye level, you can lower it to the fishing position.

**STEP 4** The two greatest faults of anglers who do not roll-cast well is that they don't allow the line to pause when they are sliding it back, so that surface tension can grip the line, and they complete their forward casts with the rod tip driving toward the water in front of them. The cast must be directed *at* the target. To prove this point to yourself, make a normal cast, directing the fly and line toward the target at about eye level. Then, make another normal cast and end the forward motion by driving the tip downward in front of you. The first cast will fly toward the target. The second will cause the front of the line to crumple into a pile, as most people's roll casts do.

## SINGLE WATER HAUL

Once the roll cast is mastered, getting more distance with a sinking line or a sinking shooting head is easy. When using a sinking line, most anglers bring in enough line so that they can make an aerial roll cast. When the fly leaves the water, they make a backcast, then a forward cast. But the backcast is made by pulling against air, which is not the best way to load a rod. The following illustrations demonstrate the single water haul, which pulls line against water tension to load the rod more effectively.

**STEP 1** To make a single water haul, make a conventional roll cast. *Be sure to direct the cast straight ahead, at eye level, as shown.*

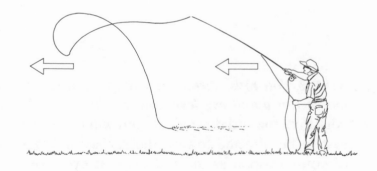

**STEP 2** *The moment the rod stops its forward motion, drop the tip toward the surface.* (If you are using a sinking line, don't allow it to drop below the surface.) The moment the line unrolls and touches the water, you are ready to make the backcast. Draw the rod back, pulling on the line while the water's surface tension is gripping it. This loads the rod for the backcast.

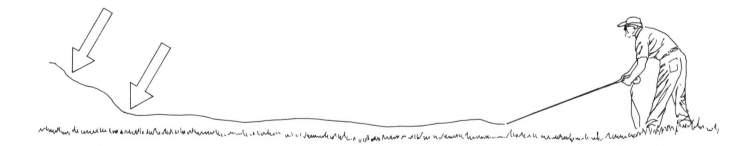

**STEP 3** The moment you feel the rod is well loaded, make a conventional backcast. Because you have loaded the rod so well by pulling against the water, you'll get a faster backcast, which will result in a longer forward cast.

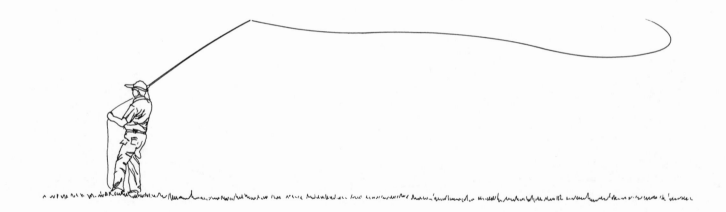

## DOUBLE WATER HAUL

An advantage of the double water haul is that on the forward cast the line travels high above the angler's body. Fly casters who have thrown lead core shooting heads and other heavy weighted lines often do what is called "the lead core lurch": The angler makes the forward cast and then ducks low, hoping the line or fly doesn't strike him. The double water haul allows you to throw the fly and line high over your head.

**STEP 1** Make a conventional roll cast and follow the procedure for making a single water haul.

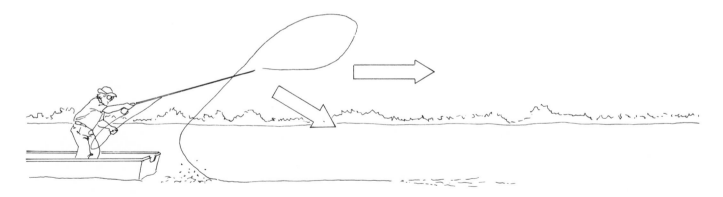

**STEP 2** Allow the line to straighten, the same as for a single water haul.

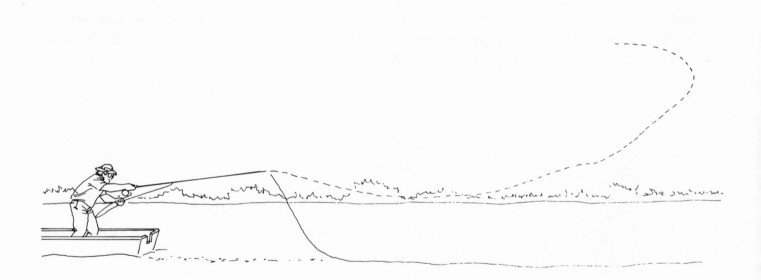

**STEP 3** Instead of making a strong backcast, make a weak one—with just enough force to lay the line softly, straight behind you. Drop the rod tip low, as shown.

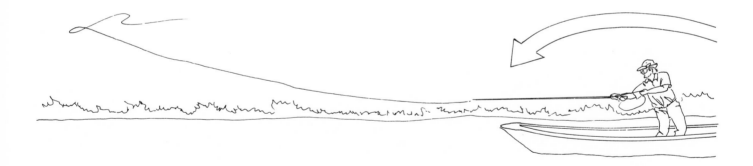

**STEP 4** Watch the line as it unrolls on the back-cast. If you're using a sinking line, don't let it drop below the surface or you won't be able to pick it up. The key is to watch the end of the line: The moment it touches the water, start a long drawing-forward motion.

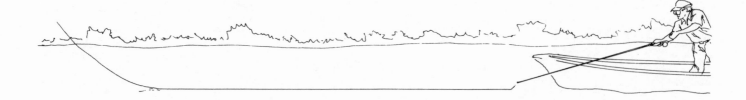

**STEP 5** When you feel the rod is well loaded, make a conventional forward cast, aiming it high overhead, as illustrated. Because you have drawn the line against the water's surface tension, you will load the rod well, and thus increase your casting distance.

# DISTANCE ROLL CAST

European anglers have been using spey casts and two-handed rods for many years to roll their lines back out for the next drift. Their technique is to place considerable line behind themselves before making the forward cast. With a conventional roll cast as practiced in the United States, very little of the line is placed back of the angler prior to the forward cast. Instead, the line is brought around beyond the angler, then the angler turns and rolls the line forward. All of this wastes energy.

A number of years ago, West Coast steelheaders adapted the spey cast for use with their single-handed rods. With this technique, an angler can roll even a weight-forward line eighty or ninety feet.

**STEP 1** Slide the line back on the surface as if you were going to make a conventional roll cast.

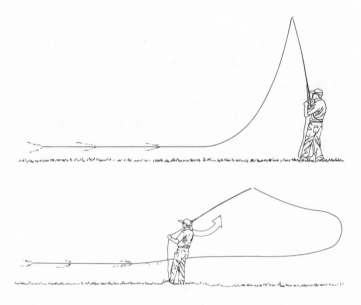

**STEP 2** This step takes practice, but it's the key to the distance roll cast. When your rod hand is about a foot in front of your face and slightly lower than your chin, lift back and up smoothly in a curved arc (note the curved arrow in the illustration). This is the angle at which you should lift the rod to drop the line behind you.

Don't go straight back, or you'll throw a weak conventional backcast. Sweeping upward and backward will lift much of the line off the water in front of you and deposit it behind you.

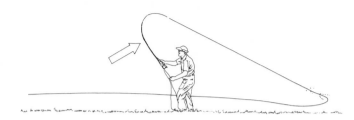

**STEP 3** *Make sure your rod extends well in back of you. As soon as the line falls to the water behind you,* make a long forward sweep to load the rod.

**STEP 4** When you feel the rod is well loaded, accelerate a short distance and stop quickly. The drawing shows the perfect place to stop on the forward cast.

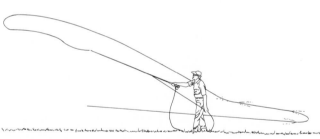

**STEP 5** The line is pulled forward easily, and a long roll cast results.

# 5

## More Distance with a Shooting Head

**A** shooting taper, which I will refer to as a shooting head, is a heavy length of fly line—usually thirty feet long—to which is attached a much thinner line. The thinner line is usually called a "shooting line." Shooting lines allow anglers to make longer casts. When released on the forward cast, the heavier head outside the rod tip drags the shooting line great distances. Distances of a hundred feet or more are common with rods size 7 or larger. All fly lines begin to fall to the water when they open and the loop unrolls. You can make shooting heads that will travel farther before opening—thus contributing to even greater distance on casts.

Use double-taper lines (they work better than forward tapers when modified as I will describe). If you are a good caster, cut thirty-five feet from one end of a double-taper line that is one size larger than the rod calls for. (For example, if you are using an 8-weight rod, use a number-9 double-taper line.) If you are not a good caster, you may want to try trimming only thirty-three or thirty-four feet. If you can handle a long line, try a forty-foot length. If you have any doubts, cut the line a little longer than I've recommended and cast it. If it seems to be unwieldy or difficult to handle, shorten it to the specifications mentioned. This is your modified shooting head.

You can attach a loop to the rear of the modified shooting head, but I have always felt that loops, no matter how small, are cumbersome and either rattle in or catch on the rod guides. However, they do offer the advantage of allowing you to change heads quickly. But if I'm using either commercial level shooting lines or braided leader material in long lengths, I prefer to permanently attach them to the rear of my shooting heads. To do this with a commercial level line, remove the finish from the end of it and the head. Sew them together with size A fly-tying thread, then overwrap the sewn area with the thread on a bobbin to make a super-smooth connection. Braided line can be slipped over the back of a modified head, then glued and wrapped, which also furnishes a very smooth connection.

There are a number of different kinds of shooting lines. Two are thin conventional fly lines. One matches a number-two level line, and the other number-three level line. The thinner line sometimes tests less than fifteen pounds, so it's not recommended for tangling with powerful fish where the leader exceeds the test of the shooting line. The larger shooting line tests above twenty-five pounds and is preferred by many people, even though a few feet of distance are sacrificed because it is a little thicker and heavier. The advantage of using these thin fly lines for shooting lines is that they handle well and rarely tangle. The disadvantage is that they are heavier than other types of shooting line.

Another kind of shooting line is made from braided leader material. Ultrafine strands of monofilament are braided into a line similar to that of the braided butt section of some leaders. The advantage of this braided line as a shooting line is that it is very limp, shoots through the guides well, and rarely tangles. The disadvantage is that it has a rough surface, and many people find that it cuts their hands.

The first shooting heads had a shooting line of monofilament. The limp monofilament used in these lines is usually of twenty- to thirty-pound test. The lighter mono is used on lines weighted 5 through 7. For saltwater fishing, heavier thirty-pound is usually preferred. Monofilament shooting lines offer several advantages. Because they have a smooth, slick surface, they shoot through the guides better than any other type. They are also thinner and lighter than other shooting lines, which allows the shooting head to travel a greater distance. They have two disadvantages: They are sometimes difficult to hold onto when fighting a fish; and because the monofilament is so light, it tends to blow around during false-casting.

# TRICKS TO HELP YOU GET MORE DISTANCE WITH A SHOOTING HEAD

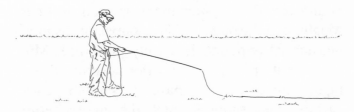

**STEP 1** The amount of shooting line falling outside the rod tip is called "overhang." To obtain maximum distance, an angler should use as much overhang as possible. The correct amount of overhang is determined by an angler's casting ability and the rod outfit used. Thus, two separate anglers using the same outfit will use different lengths of overhang. And one angler with two different outfits may need four feet of overhang with one rod and five feet with the other. To determine if you have a correct amount of overhang, extend two to three feet of shooting line outside the rod tip. With the rod tip low to the water, begin a backcast.

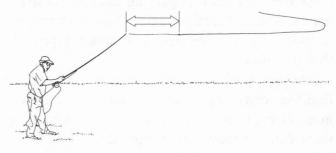

**STEP 2** Make several false casts and watch your shooting head. As long as you do not have too much overhang, the line will unroll smoothly, as shown.

**STEP 3** Gradually work out more overhang, because additional overhang will increase your distance potential. The moment you have too much overhang, you will see your shooting head begin to vibrate. This is because the thinner shooting line cannot support the heavy head.

**STEP 4** Gradually retract the length of overhang until the vibrations disappear. The point at which the vibrating stops indicates the greatest length of overhang you can handle with that particular outfit. Now you are ready to make the final backcast.

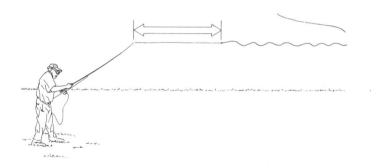

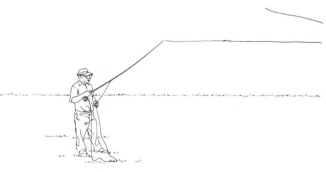

**STEP 5** To obtain greater distance, add one more trick. As the *last* backcast is made, shoot as much line behind you as is equal to the length of your overhang. Then trap the line, and come forward hauling as you do so. By shooting this extra line on the backcast, you can add many feet to your final forward cast.

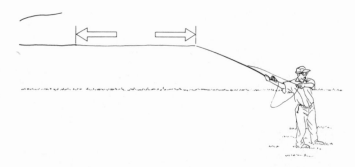

# 6

## Special Casting Problems

## THE LONG-LINE PICKUP

**A** major problem for many casters is picking up a long line lying on the water's surface. Most anglers begin experiencing problems at about forty feet. When you understand *why* this is so difficult, and how to overcome the problem, lifting even eighty feet of line from the surface won't be too hard for you.

Surface tension grips a fly line that is floating on the water—it doesn't want to let the line go. That's why it is so important to stop the line as you take it back to make a roll cast. This stop allows surface tension to grasp the line so the rod has something to pull against to load itself. Surface tension is a plus factor with a roll cast, but with a conventional backcast it will inhibit your attempt to lift a long line from the surface.

In making a long-line pickup, all fly line must be removed from the water before the backcast is begun.

*It is also important that the pickup starts with the rod tip touching the water.* The higher the tip is off the surface when you begin a backcast, the less amount of line you can lift. Follow the four steps shown here, and you'll be able to lift large amounts of line from the surface.

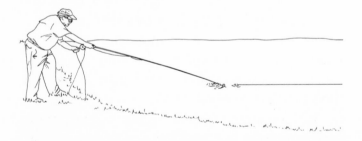

**STEP 1** Lower the rod tip to the water, pointing it in the direction of the fly. Bend over and lean

forward: This allows you to lift a little more line than you could from an upright position. Use your line hand to remove all slack from the line.

**STEP 2** As soon as all slack has been removed, reach forward and grasp the line as close as you can to the butt or stripping guide.

**STEP 3** Raise the rod, *but try to keep your line hand in the position you started with—close to the butt guide.* When you think you have lifted as much line from the surface as you can, pull

downward with the line hand, which will allow
you to lift even more of the line. At this point,
if you have made all the right moves, most of
the fly line will lift from the surface, and only
the leader and fly will remain there.

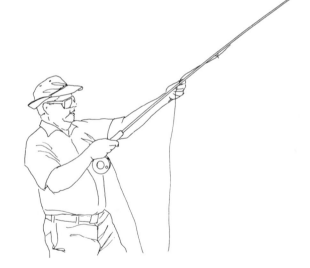

**STEP 4** Make a normal backcast. You will need
to use a single haul, and of course another haul
on the forward cast.

## CASTING WITH THE WIND AT YOUR BACK

Many fly casters curse the wind, but when the wind is at your back it can help you make a longer cast—if you use it to your advantage. If you can make a tight loop on the backcast, the wind at your back will help you cast longer than you normally could.

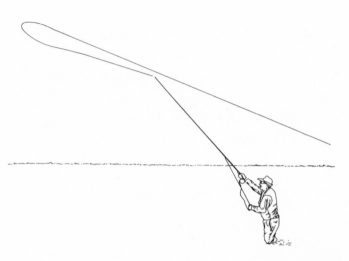

**STEP 1** Make a low, tight-loop backcast to the side that tilts slightly downward but doesn't hit the water behind you.

**STEP 2** Make the forward cast at an upward angle, as shown. The line will be carried forward by the wind a great distance. The higher the angle the cast is directed, the more the wind will assist in carrying the line forward. In effect, you have turned the line into a kite for the wind to push. Once you master this cast, you will throw more line than your reel can hold.

## CASTING INTO THE WIND

The major problem with casting into the wind is that once the line straightens, it tends to be blown back until the leader falls in a tangled mess. The key is to throw the cast so that the fly is aimed directly at the target. As soon as the line straightens, the fly falls to the surface and cannot be blown back. It helps to make the tightest loop you possibly can—which means making the shortest acceleration coupled with a quick stop at the end of the cast—to throw the line into the teeth of the wind.

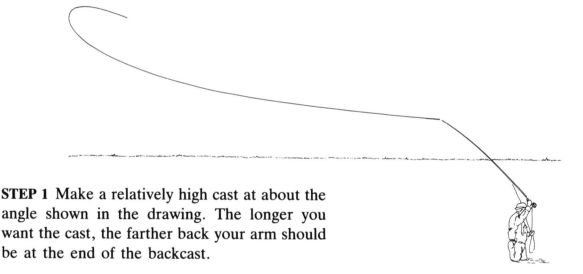

**STEP 1** Make a relatively high cast at about the angle shown in the drawing. The longer you want the cast, the farther back your arm should be at the end of the backcast.

**STEP 2** On the forward cast, direct the line so the fly is driven right at the target area. Your goal is to deliver the cast so the fly touches the surface when the leader unrolls. Then the wind will not be able to blow the line and fly backward.

# WIND BLOWING TOWARD THE ROD SIDE OF THE ANGLER

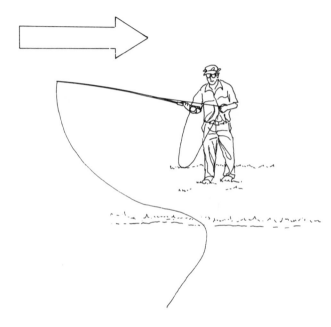

One of the most frustrating things that can happen when you are fly casting is wind blowing directly against your rod side. This makes it possible for the fly or line to hit you on both the back and forward casts. Some anglers will try to cast backhanded in this situation, but that's not very satisfactory because such a cast restricts natural arm motions and makes for inefficient casting. The best way to eliminate the problem is to learn to cast with either hand. When there is a wind on the right, simply switch the rod to your left hand. But because most fly fishermen aren't going to do that, here is a method to help you defeat the wind.

**STEP 1** Lower the rod tip to the surface, and point it at the fly. Then begin a sidearm cast, as shown. This will carry the line well away from you, so it won't hit you on the backcast.

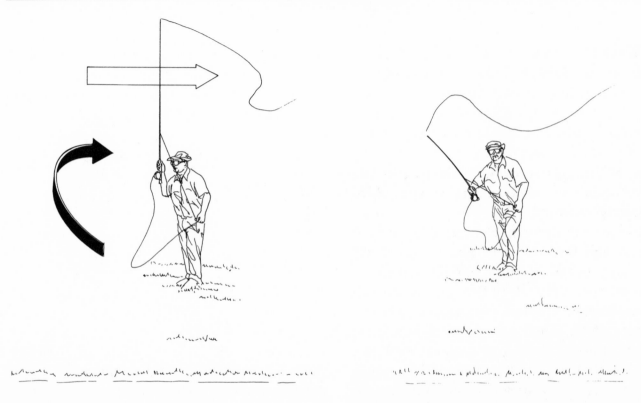

**STEP 2** As soon as the backcast ends, sweep the rod in toward your body.

**STEP 3** Make a conventional forward cast, with one difference. You know the wind is going to blow the line, so count on it! Don't tilt the rod slightly, as we usually do on a forward cast. Instead, during the very last stages of the cast *make sure the rod travels perfectly vertically.* The breeze will cause the line to blow downwind of you, and it will pass harmlessly by. Finish the cast as you would any normal forward cast.

## THE CHANGE-OF-DIRECTION CAST

There are many fishing situations where you need to make a quick change of direction after the cast has been started. Perhaps a trout rises to one side or a bass crashes against some reeds to your left or right, and you need to get the fly there immediately. Or you have cast slightly upcurrent in a river and the fly has drifted

downstream: You then want to return the fly to the point where you started the first drift. Such casts are easy to make with a moderate amount of line—up to about forty feet.

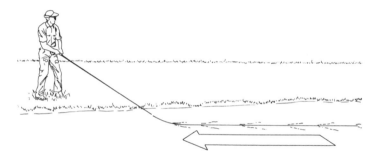

**STEP 1** With the rod to your left, let's say a cast directly to the front is desired. Hold the

rod inches above the water, and sweep the rod tip to the side, drawing the line along the water. You want to keep as much line on the water as possible to aid in loading the rod on the backcast.

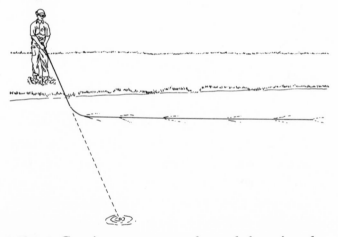

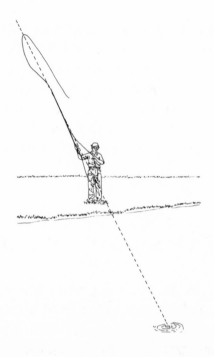

**STEP 2** Continue to sweep the rod, keeping the tip low to the surface, until it is pointing at the target area.

**STEP 3** As soon as the rod tip points at the target, make a backcast directly opposite the target. It is vital that you don't stop when the rod tip points at the target. If you stop, the line end will stop, and you'll have difficulty making the cast.

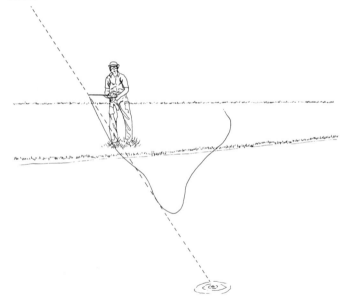

**STEP 4** As soon as the backcast unrolls, make a conventional forward cast to the target.

## THE RIGHT-ANGLE CAST

A problem that comes up frequently for trout fishermen, and occasionally for other anglers, is that a cast is needed when there is a high obstruction direct behind them. This is where a right-angle cast helps. Such a cast can only be made well to about thirty-five feet, but casts within that distance can be made with less than five feet of clearance behind.

**STEP 1** Stand parallel to the obstruction and make a normal backcast. Be sure to extend your rod hand well behind your body.

**STEP 2** Bring your rod hand forward until it is even with your body. Remember, the line will go in the direction that the rod tip is pointing after it accelerates and stops. So at this point, move your casting hand ninety degrees to the side, so that it points at the target.

**STEP 3** Don't start accelerating your rod hand until the right-angle turn toward the target is made. Finish the acceleration and stop with the rod tip pointing in the direction you want the fly to go. You'll find the line sweeps forward alongside the obstruction behind you, then turns at a right angle and drops the fly where you want it.

# WHEN THERE IS LITTLE BACKCAST ROOM

When you have only a little backcast room, twenty-five feet, for example, you can still make a cast to fifty or more feet in front of you. The key is not to make a standard backcast, which travels fast and straight behind. Instead, make a *circular* backcast—one that travels in a large oval.

**STEP 1** Before making the actual cast, practice this little technique to help learn the cast quicker. Allow about twelve feet of line to extend beyond the rod tip. Begin rotating your rod hand in a circle. Keep continuous pressure on the line as your hand travels around the circle. This will force the rod to constantly pull on the line, and the line will follow the path in which the tip travels. If you do this properly, the line should travel as shown in the drawing. Once you master this trick, making a backcast when there is little room will be no problem.

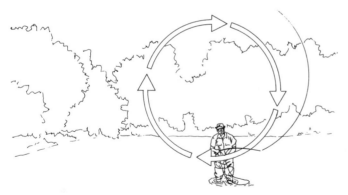

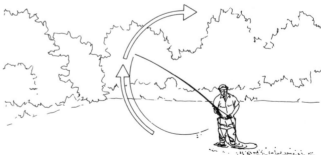

**STEP 2** If you have an obstruction behind you about twenty-five feet, put out about thirty or thirty-five feet of line. Make a backcast by rotating the rod hand in a half-circle, as shown. Be sure you apply constant rod pressure on the line around the half-circle. Because the line will be traveling in a circle to the side, none of it will touch the obstruction.

**STEPS 3 AND 4** When the rod reaches the point directly above your head, accelerate your rod hand quickly toward the target to make a tight loop. It pays to make a single haul at this point. If you make the cast correctly, you will have generated enough line speed so that you can shoot another fifteen to thirty feet of line to the target. With some practice, you'll be able to throw your fly a considerable distance with little room for your backcast.

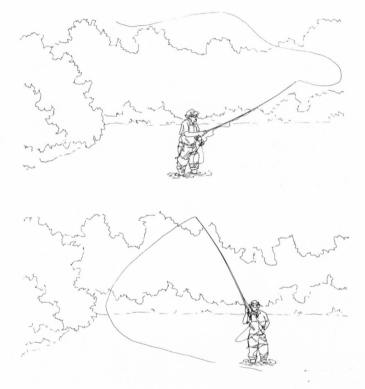

# THROWING AN EXTRA-HIGH BACKCAST, OR A BACKCAST INTO AN OPENING

There are times when a high bank, trees, or a wall is behind an angler. A high backcast is needed to get the line and fly above the obstruction. There are also occasions where there is an opening in the trees to the rear, and if the angler could backcast into the opening, he could make a longer forward cast.

What most anglers try to do in these situations is to make a conventional backcast above the obstruction or into the opening. This strategy usually ends in disaster because the line is going to travel in the direction the hand is aiming when it stops at the end of the cast. If you make a backcast in the normal manner and try to throw it higher, your hand points on the stop in the direction of the obstruction. And if you try to throw your normal backcast into a small opening in the trees, you most likely will throw a wider loop and end up with your fly caught in the trees.

Here is an improved method that allows you to throw longer backcasts and higher ones, too. It also allows a much more accurate cast into an opening.

**STEP 1** How you start the cast is important. Touch the rod tip to the water, as shown. Invert your rod hand so that the rod is held upside down, with the reel pointing up and your thumb on the down side. With your thumb underneath like this, you can stop your hand on the acceleration at a much higher angle. And for casting into an opening, you'll essentially be making a forward cast behind you. Almost all anglers make a better, more controlled forward cast than they do a backcast—so this method improves their chances of throwing the fly into an opening behind them.

**STEP 2** You should never make a backcast until you get the end of the line moving and all line off the water. Regardless of the amount of line on the surface when you start the cast, if you lift the rod tip smoothly and swiftly, by the time your rod hand has reached the position in the drawing, all line will be off the surface.

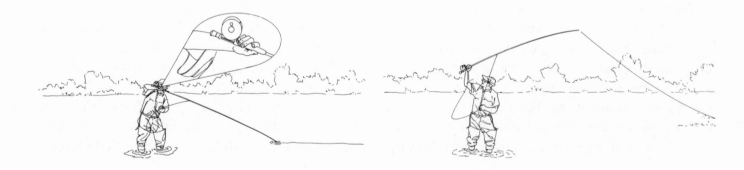

**STEP 3** Accelerate the rod tip and stop when the tip points in the direction you want to go—either above the obstruction, or into an opening.

**STEP 4** As soon as the stop is made, rotate your hand back to a normal position.

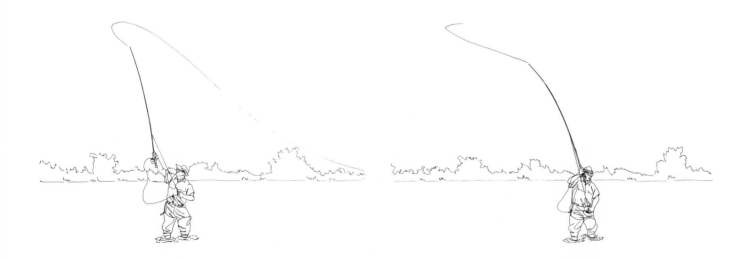

**STEP 5** Bring the rod forward to get the end moving, as you would for a normal forward cast.

**STEP 6** Finish as you would a normal forward cast.

## CONTROLLING LINE ON THE SHOOT

**VIEW 1** This is how many anglers release line on the shoot, allowing it to flow uncontrolled.

A major mistake made by many, even experienced, fly fishermen when they throw a long line is to let go of it with the line hand. Three undesirable things can happen if the line is allowed to shoot uncontrolled through the guides.

One, because the line is flowing freely, it will often wrap around the rod guide or, worse, the handle or the reel. Two, if the line is released, its flight cannot be controlled. Three, when the line touches the surface, the angler has no control until it is recovered. Should a strike occur, or the fly need to be manipulated, the angler is unprepared.

**VIEW 2** By forming a ring with the thumb and first finger of the line hand and holding it around the shooting line below the first guide, the angler maintains control throughout the line's flight. At any time, the fly can be stopped and dropped on the target. The line doesn't have a chance to tangle with the rod; and when the fly settles to the water, instant control of it is insured.

## CONTROLLING A LONG LINE WHEN WADING

When you are fishing a longer line and are forced to retrieve while wading, you may have a problem handling the line stripped in during that retrieve. If you're standing in current, the line will be swept downstream and have to be yanked back before anything can be done with it. And when wading for bonefish, the line will trail along behind you, and will have to be recovered before it can be cast. There is a method that allows you to retrieve at least thirty feet of line and keep it under control. It takes a little practice to master, but once learned is a blessing.

**VIEW 1** The cast has been made and the retrieve begins. When about ten feet of line have been recovered, slide the line back to the joint between the thumb and index finger on your line hand and trap it there. So the line doesn't slip, close the joint firmly.

**VIEW 2** Continue to strip in line. When approximately ten more feet of line have been recovered, trap the line between the middle joint of your thumb and your index finger. By pressing your thumb against your first finger, you'll hold the line securely while you continue to strip more line. When another ten feet of line is taken in, trap it with the end of your thumb against your index finger.

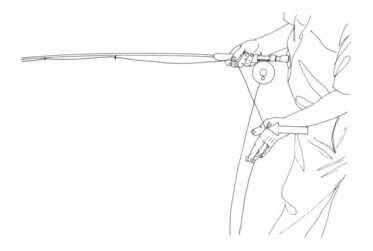

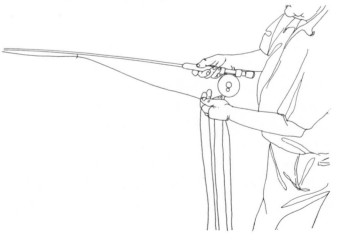

**VIEW 3** You are now ready to make a backcast. If you've kept your thumb pressed against your index finger, all three coils of line will be under control during casting.

**VIEW 4** Come forward after your backcast to make a forward cast. Until you become proficient with this method, it's a good idea to make the forward cast, shoot the topmost coil, make a backcast, and on a final forward cast shoot the other two coils. Once you have mastered the cast, you can end the stripping retrieve,

make a backcast and shoot the first coil (using a double haul to help you), and shoot the other two coils as you come forward. In other words, in a single back and forward cast, you'll be able to shoot the line while keeping the length of retrieved line under control.

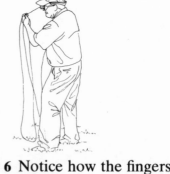

**VIEWS 5 AND 6** Notice how the fingers are held open to allow the line to flow off on the final forward cast.

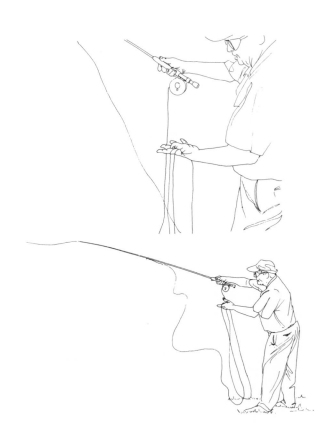

# THE BASEBALL THROW

This versatile cast allows you to do several things. First, it will let you throw a dry fly into the teeth of the wind with authority. You'll be surprised how well you can turn over even an eleven- or twelve-foot leader in a stiff breeze. Second, there are many times when a long cast must be made, but the line and fly have to be kept close to the water. An example would be throwing well back under a pier or dock, or driving a fly under an overhanging bush at the water's edge. And third, there are situations in which an angler may want to throw a long line into a stiff wind while keeping line and fly close to the surface throughout their flight. The Baseball Throw is the cast for all these situations. I chose that name because you make this cast close to the way you throw a baseball. On a very short ball toss, the throwing hand doesn't go back very far. But when you want to make a long throw, you pull your hand well in back of your body—as you will in this cast.

**STEP 1** Begin a backcast so that your arm is fully extended, as shown. God rarely lets us make a perfect backcast, so we must remove any slack before we move the fly. An asset of this cast is that you can remove more slack than you would with a conventional backcast.

**STEP 2** Here is where this cast differs from almost all other conventional casting motions. The rod is carried forward and remains parallel to the water surface until your hand is even with your shoulder. This is one of the very few casts where I recommend you bend your wrist during the cast—it is necessary in order to bring the rod forward while keeping it parallel to the water.

**STEP 3** The angler is turning back toward the target while drawing his rod forward. When the angler is facing the target and the rod hand has come even with his shoulder, he should straighten his wrist and raise his elbow until it is just below the shoulder. Forearm and hand now travel parallel to the ground and straight forward. Unless you use this motion, you won't be able to make the cast properly.

**STEP 4** The wrist is now straight and the thumb is on top of the rod handle. At this point, make an incredibly short and high-speed acceleration—*being sure that the tip travels exactly parallel to the surface toward the target area.* Then come to a quick stop. If the rod is accelerated at an up or down angle, the line will travel up or down. But if the tip accelerates parallel to the surface, and straight ahead, the line will travel at that angle. Remember this important principle: *The line is going to go in the direction the tip is accelerated and where it stops.*

# BRIEF INDEX